For Steve

Any resemblance to the CSO is purely coincidental.

Court & Lynn

POST EARLY
Hoffnung

THE HOFFNUNG SYMPHONY ORCHESTRA

By the Author of

THE MAESTRO
THE HOFFNUNG SYMPHONY ORCHESTRA
THE HOFFNUNG COMPANION TO MUSIC
HOFFNUNG'S MUSICAL CHAIRS
HOFFNUNG'S ACOUSTICS

The Hoffnung Symphony Orchestra

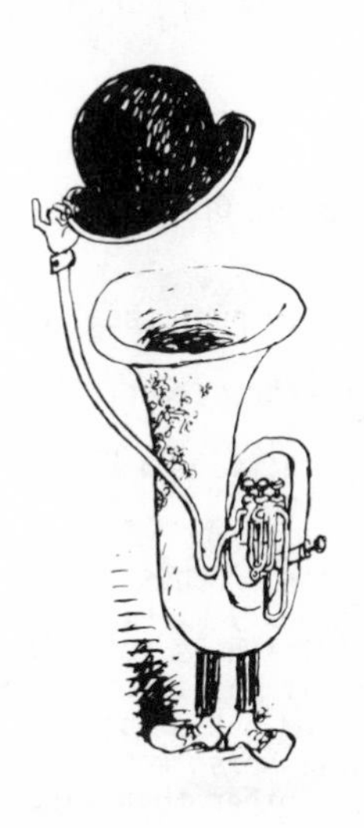

by
Gerard Hoffnung

Riverrun Press · New York

This edition published by Riverrun Press,
Inc., 175 Fifth Avenue, New York, N.Y. 10010

First published by Dennis Dobson 1955

ISBN: 0 86676 008 3

Library of Congress Catalog Card Number:
83-22916

Library of Congress Cataloging in Publication Data

Hoffnung, Gerard.
The Hoffnung Symphony Orchestra.

Cartoons.
Reprint. Originally published: London :
Dobson, 1955.
1. Symphony orchestras--Caricatures and
cartoons. I. Title.
ML87.H65 1984 741.5'942 83-22916
ISBN 0-86676-008-3 (pbk.)

THE STRINGS

The Violin (Leader)

The Violon Double

The Viola

The Viola Pizzicato

The Yo-Bow

The Cello

The Double Bass (a left handed player)

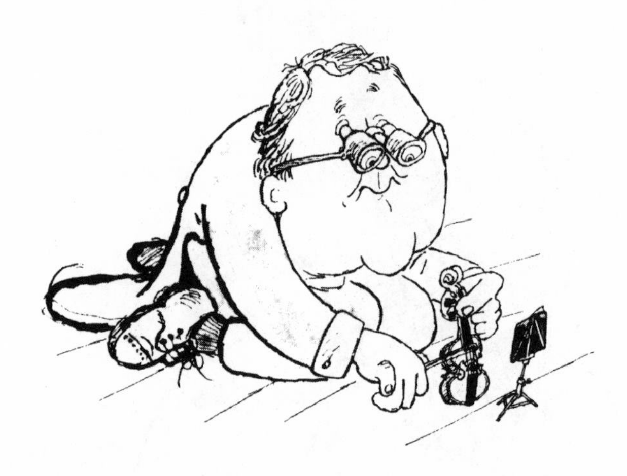

The Piccolo Double Bass

The Harp

The String Tuba

This instrument is sometimes referred to as the "Minstrel Tuba" or the "Blow-Plucker". It is interesting to note that the String Tuba is a member of both the string and brass families though it is usually seated with the former.

The Zither

The Piano (Boudoir Grand)

The Spanish Guitar

The Ondes Martenot

THE WOODWIND

The Flute and the Piccolo Flute

The Bass Flute

SUITE

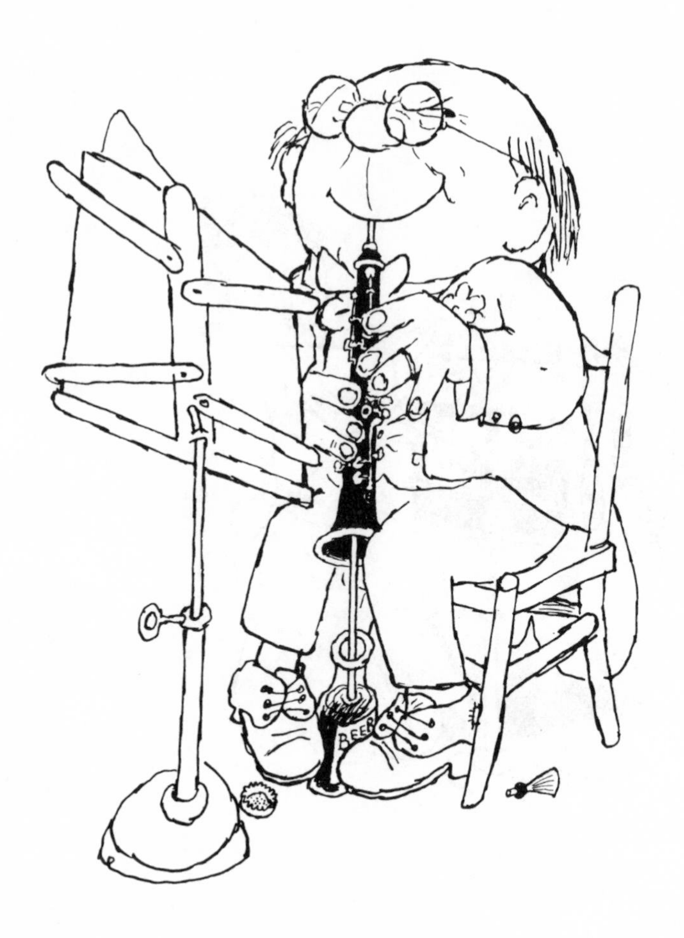

The Oboe

The Cor Anglais

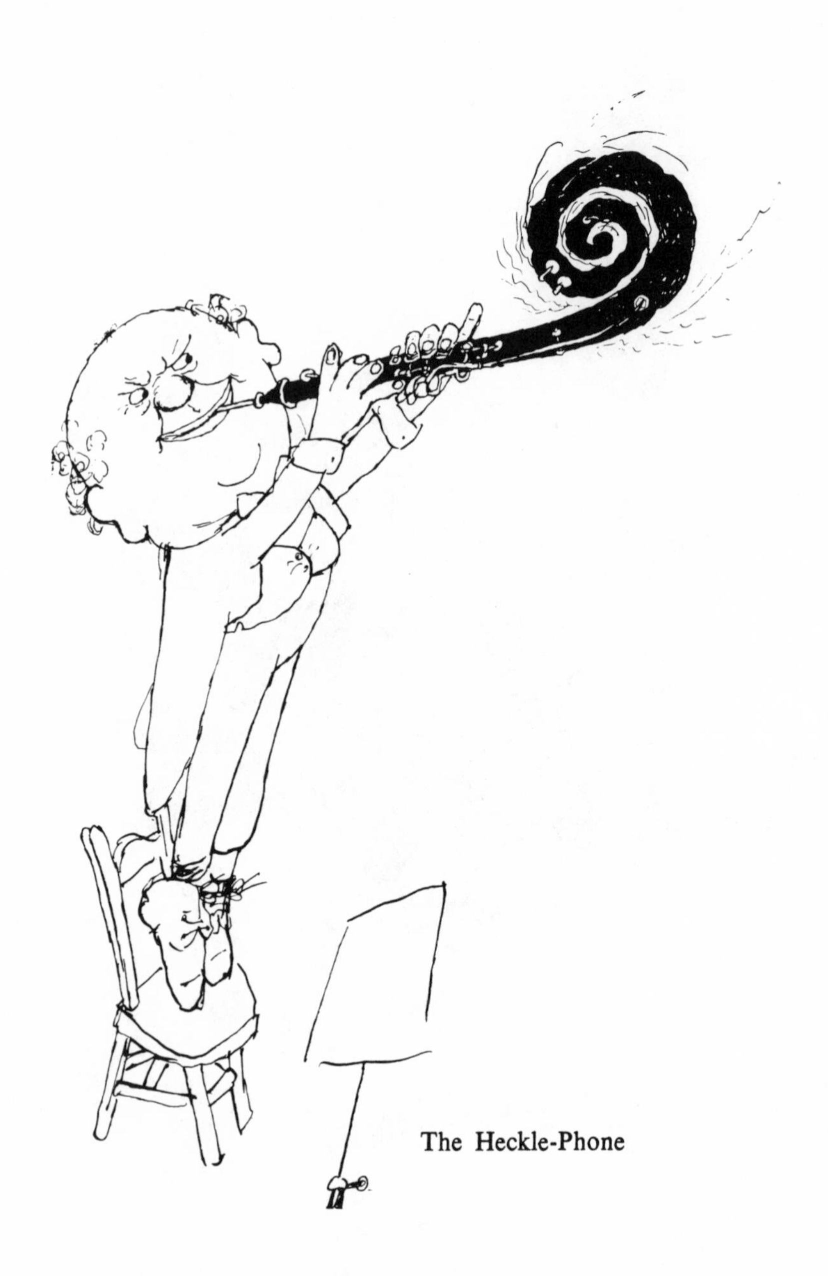

The Heckle-Phone

The Clarinet and the Bass Clarinet

The Saxophone

The Bassethorn

The Bassoon

The Contra-Bassoon

The Organ

THE BRASS

The Horn

The Trinkler

The Double Trumpet

The Serpent

For security reasons this instrument is no longer in use.

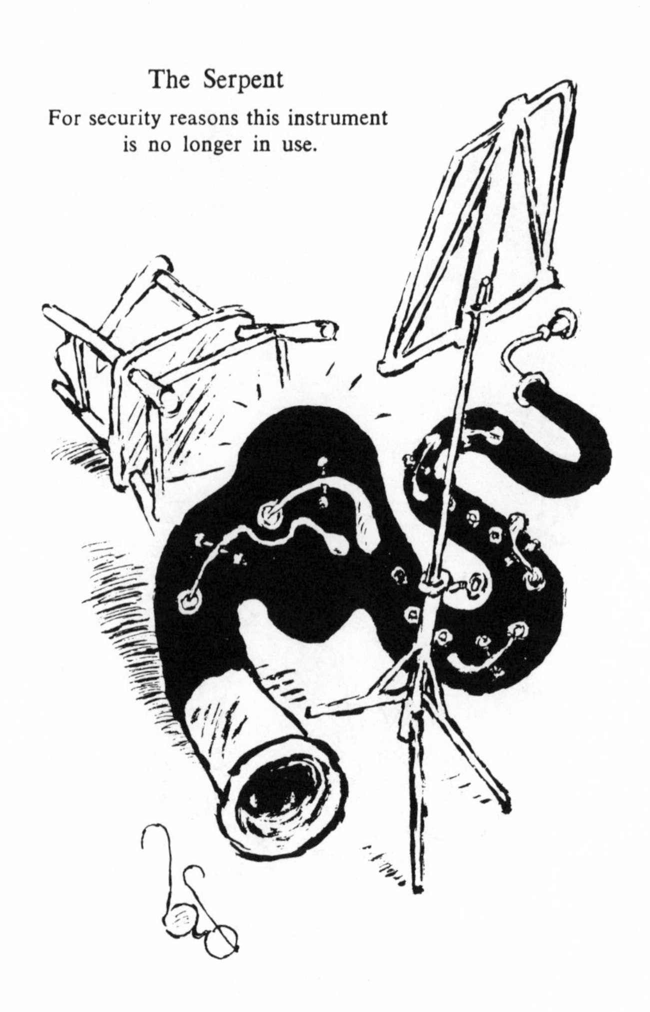

The Trombone

The Bass Trombone

The Wagner Tuba

The Bass Tuba

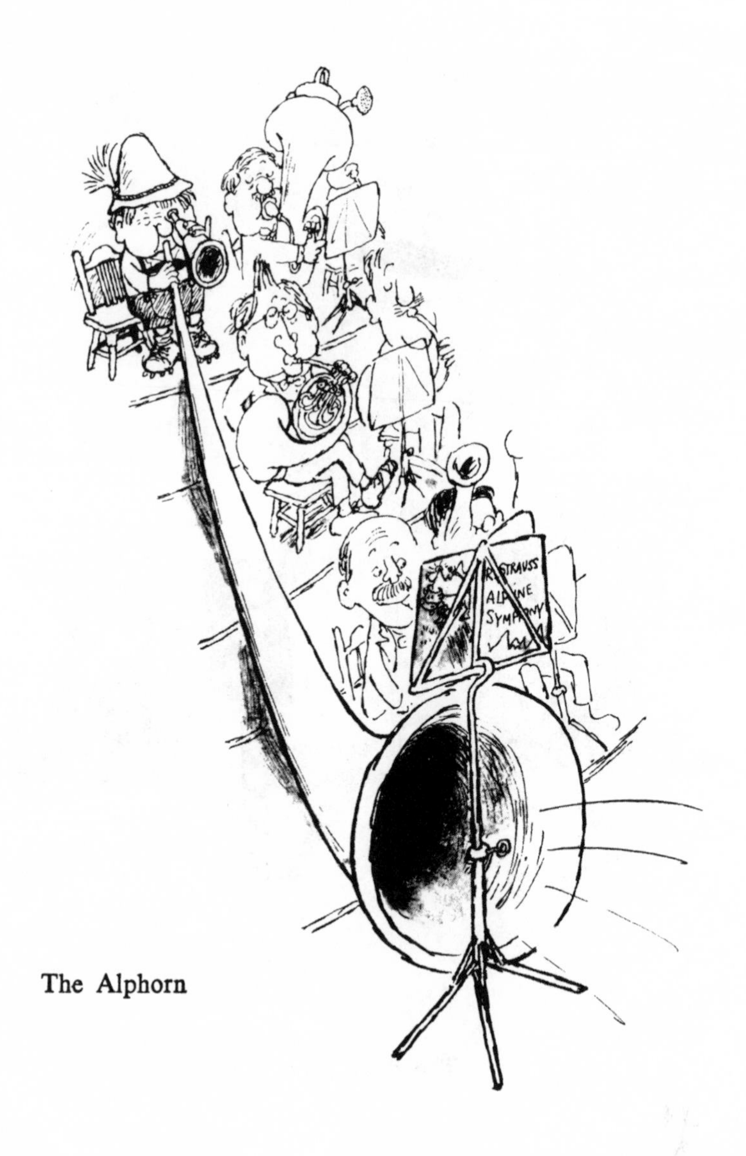

The Alphorn

THE PERCUSSION

The Timpani

The Cymbals

The Side Drum

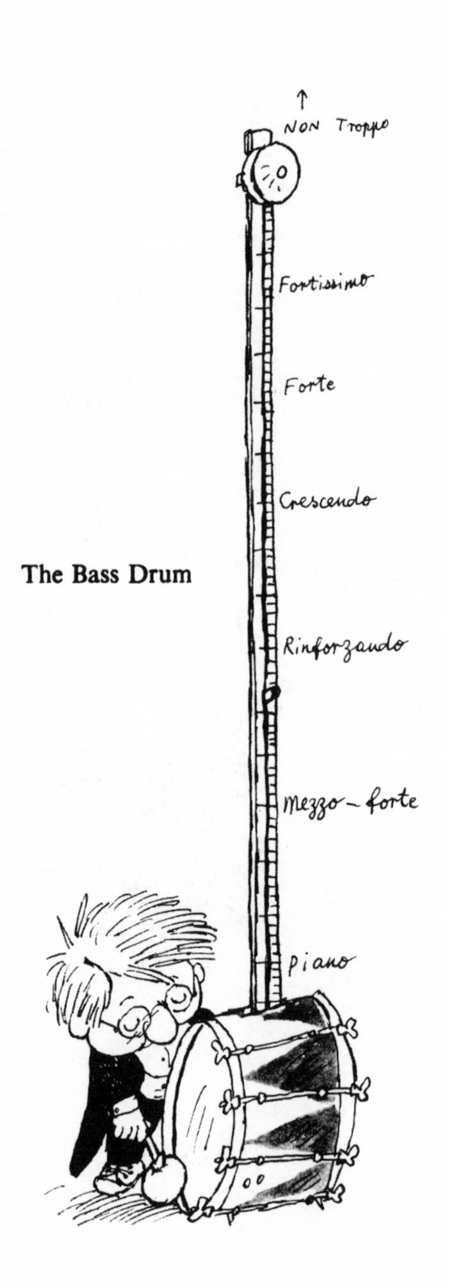

The Bass Drum

The Tum Drum

The Tubular Bells

The Triangle

The Xylophone

The Vibraphone

The Celeste

The Jingle Bells and the Chinese Block

The Wind Machine

Don Quixote
by
Richard Strauss

The Gong and the Tam Tam

The Castanets

END

POST EARLY
Hoffnung